Cont

MY LIFE

AND

POEMS

PATRICIA PAGE

Fantine Press

First published 2008
by

FANTINE PRESS
The Coach House
Stansted Hall
Stansted
Essex CM24 8UD

ISBN 978 1 901958 19 5

Printed in England by Booksprint

I was born in Liverpool, England in 1943 in my grandmothers house in the district called Knotty Ash, which is also the home of the famous comedian Ken Dodd who still lives there. I never used to read *Psychic News* although my mother Deborah did. One day in 1990 my mother said "The *Psychic News* want poems." At first I didn't take much notice. I had never written a poem in my life. I went to my bedroom and let my imagination roll. My first poem is called *An Appreciation.*

It is dedicated to my dear mother Debbie, with much love and affection. If she had not mentioned that *Psychic News* wanted poems, I wouldn't have written one, because I didn't read *Psychic News* then or anything like that. I'll always be grateful to my mother because without her help I would never have known that I could write poetry.

AN APPRECIATION

When we think of the sun
we think of the warmth and having fun
It makes the plants and flowers grow
To make us happy when we are feeling low
Beautiful flowers like the rose and the poppy
beautiful things that artists like to copy
The beautiful rainbow, a colourful show
The beautiful sea, God’s TV
For us to share
A beautiful Earth for us to love and treat with care
Beautiful trees and the grass is green
Twinkling stars and the moon at night can be seen
I hope you enjoyed this little rhyme
I would like to write more but I am running out of time.

LIFE'S MYSTERIES

At night time we look at the sky,
And see a star so near yet so far away,
Then in daytime like magic appears the colourful rainbow
But where does it go?
Then beyond the sky, does God sit on his throne?
Is He our Father, is heaven our proper home?
Then the sky, sometimes grey, sometimes blue,
God made these wonderful thungs for me and you,
the trees so tall and the leaves so green,
and the grass like green carpets that have to be seen,
and the beautiful colours of plants and flowers,
They belong to God but they are also ours
Some flowers are red, some yellow, some pink.
They die but come back to life, it make one think,
Then God's creatures, a bird, acat or a dog,
The elements, the rain and snow and fog,
Like magic they appear but where do they go?
Like the warm sun, and the cold winds that blow'
It must be part of God's plan'
So we must be kind to one another whenever we can,
Does God give us a reward?
With God around we cannot be lonely or bored.

THE FOUR SEASONS

I wonder why we have four seasons?
God must have his reasons.
Just like when we are born and when we die,
Do we go to heaven beyond the sky?
And the stars that come out and twinkle at night,
where do they go when it is daylight?
And the cold white snow it comes but only to disappear,
But on Chistmas cards with the robin it fills us full of
Christmas cheer,
And the beautiful tulips and daffodils come out in spring
And the world is happy and the birds sing,
Then summer comes nice warm sunshine
And the beautiful green grass and trees,
Then autumn comes the leaves start falling,
The weather goes cold
But like us and the four seasons and God
We never really get old.

THE HEATWAVE

In 1976, the year of the heatwave,
My parents and I went on holiday to Devon,
The weather was lovely, we thought it was heaven,
Then after a week we stepped inside the train
Like from a dream to reality, a quick change so strange,
we passed some cows gathered under a tree'
to keep cool, they were no fool,
Tenyears after my Dad passed away,
Mum and I have happy memories of Devon.
I suppose Dad has gone to heaven,
In the early hours I saw a cat,
it can be seen but can't be heard,
of getting chased or attacked, it can't be scared.
Then the sound of the early morning bus,
The pussycat makes for home without a fuss,
Then comes the milkman on his daily round,
Next the postman delivers the letters as his feet
make a heavy sound on the ground,
Then a dog begins to bark,
The birds are singing in the park,
Day has begun.
Let's hope it stays full of happiness and fun.

GOD'S CREATURES

My sister has a cat called Lucy,
Gosh, and she is very choosy,
My friend had a dog called Ted,
He would let you know when he had not been fed,
Then there were two budgies Joey and Soey. They died.
Now they will be swinging in heaven side by side.
Then there is Tim, the circus horse.
He loves the people and the applause.
Then there are the lovely goldfish,
They swim so free in their bowl by a pretty pink dish.
The sparrows keep on chirping happily,
Even when the weather is cold,
the pigeons walk around
Looking for food in all kinds of weather so bold.
Then there is the elephant so big and strong,
and the swan with its beautiful neck so white and long,
and the beautiful zebra looks like a striped horse,
that has been painted by God,
These are all creatures of God.
Big and small
and short and tall
Even you and I are all beautiful in God's eyes.

DREAMS

I dreamed I was talking to my dad
but when I awoke, he died in 1986,
it makes me sad
When we dream we don’t plan the scene.
Sometimes they are happy
sometimes they are sad.
The people we see, some are good, some are bad
The colours , the flowers, the people are real,
but when we awake, it would seem
that was only a dream,
Then it’s gone forever
God must be very clever
Friends and relations we see live and die,
but God lets us all meet again
in His heaven beyond the sky.

THE SHOPPING TROLLEY

There is a lady called Mary who is very jolly
she went to the shops to show off her new shopping trolley
her friends said it must have cost a high price
"I won it at Bingo," Mary said,
her friends replied, "oh very nice."
Mary went into the supermarket
to buy food for her cat Ted,
he was always in a better mood when he had been fed,
then mary bought some cakes and pop,
for friends coming to tea,
and Mary thought the big cake is for me,
Mary started to go home, she thought,
I hope I haven't missed anybody on the phone
halfway down the lane it started to rain
Mary started to run and thought I am having fun,
Mary opened her door,
there on the floor was Ted
waiting to be fed.
Mary set the table for tea
when the clock struck four
there was a knock at the door,
it was Mary's friends with their children,
they all enjoyed the cakes and lemonade for tea,
they all had a happy chat and watched TV,
then time to go home Mary said don't forget to phone,
so Mary and Ted had a happy day,
then the moon and stars came out to play.

Chapter 1

My Mother and Father

My mother was the eldest of eleven children. She had pneumonia twice when she was a child. They really thought she was going to die. She was flaxen but went bald. When her hair grew again it was dark. She had to learn to read and write all over again. There was one teacher with black rimmed glasses, her hair in a bun, very strict. My mother was frightened of her. My mother didn't do well at school at first. Then she got a different teacher. My mother said she was lovely and patient . My mother started to pick up again and very soon learned to read and write. Her auntie bought her a lovely Bible, my mother said, but her two younger sisters soon took posession of that. She had to share a bed with her two sisters. One Christmas my mother said the nice teacher took her and another girl out of the class to see a pantomime down town and the grotto. My mother said on their way back home the teacher drove them down a street called Everystreet. The teacher turned to them and smiled, "Now you can always say you have been down every street in Liverpool."

When the war was on my mother worked in a bread shop. Once a week she would go to the cinema. In the blackout, it would flash on the screen "stay at your own risk." She always stayed till the end of the picture because she could not stand being in the air raid shelter. She had claustrophobia and had to be in the open air. One night she said she was walking home from the cinema and she heard footsteps behind her. She started to run back home and when she got nearer home she could hear her father's voice saying "What silly fool is out on a night like this?" One of the neighbours said "It's your Debbie." They were all in the air raid shelter in the garden. My mother made them all cups of hot cocoa. Her brother Jack was on leave from the merchant navy. He was always asleep when the air raids were on. She said to her mother "Jack won't come to the shelter" "Oh, just leave him, my grandmother said.

My mother said when she got back from the cinema she used to tell her two younger sisters everything she had seen at the cinema. Then they would go to sleep.

My father George was the youngest of fourteen children. he said one night when he was on leave from the army he was walking home and heard somebody running. It might have been my mother and the footsteps she heard could have been my father. He only lived around the corner from her. They started courting and got married. They were living in rooms.

Chapter 2

My Early Life

My father was a plumber. I was born in my grandmother's house in Knotty Ash. Then I had a sister Jean but she died of pneumonia when she was nine months old. Then my mother had another baby called Georgina. My father managed to get a big old house in Ivy Leigh. We moved there when I was two. When I was five, on my first day at school, I remember it was playtime. The girls gates were chained and locked, but the boys were not so I sneaked into the boys playground and ran all the way home. I stood in the path, my mother was paying the insurance man when she saw me and took me back to school. If she had not, I wouldn't have learned to read and write.

When I was six years of age my brother George was born. When it was the queen's coronationthere was a party. It was a street party which was great fun. We were all sitting at a big long table full of sandwiches and cakes. Then it started to rain. At the end of the week all the children in the street went to the cinema. We had our photographs taken. At school every week we gave a shilling to the teacher. When it was getting nearer the coronation it paid for our trip to London. When we arrived in London it was a hot day and there were crowds everywhere. We were walking round with the two teachers from two classes. We stopped at a cafe and had a nice meal and orange juice but coming back on the train I felt faint and sick. It was a good job my friend Jean was with me. She lived in the same street as me.

When I was thirteen years old I won two tickets from the *Girls Crystal* comic. The prize was to see Joan Regan, the singer and Brian Reece in a pantomime at the Empire Theatre. My sister and I went and we had to stand outside wearing *Girl's Crystal* badges. We were all given a bag of chocolates.

My mother said she was born in her grandmothers house in everton. Her grandmother was only sixteen when she was married to a London businessman twice her age. His family finished with him so he bought two houses in Everton.

My mother said when her father was small, he used to have to polish the silver and swill the yard before he went to school – his father was strict. When he grew up he married my mother's mother.

My mother said when she was courting she used to go to my father's house, my grandmother on my father's side used to be shouting at my grand dad saying "Oh, you and your Welsh sisters." My mother said she used to like going to their house – as she had a good laugh.

Chapter 3

Womanhood

I got married when I was twenty. I was a waitress in a cafe down town and my husband to be came in every morning for beans on toast with his friend. He was a window cleaner. I was only courting for two months before getting married. We were living in rooms when I became pregnant. One time he pushed me down the stairs. I knocked on the flat below. Cathy lived there with her five children. I stayed there for a while. I had a baby boy but he died when he was two months oldfrom acute bronchitis. I started living with my mother again and got divorced in 1967.

Another time I got a job with Butlins holiday camp for a few months then I came back to Liverpool and moved into an unfurnished flat. My mother bought me some seconhand furniture and I got a job in a sweet factory.I saved up and bought myself a beautiful grey coat with big silver buttons. My flat was at the top of a big old house with cellars. One day I came back from doing a bit of shopping when I heard scratching and scampering of feet coming from my room. It was rats! I went to the council and told them I was getting no sleep, and I had to go to work. They offered me a flat in Kirkby. It was on the third floor but I took it because I was desperate. I thought "Well there are no rats here so I should get some sleep."

Another time I used to have to get the bus to the town centre to sign on at the labour exchange. One morning I was late. I looked at the clock and there wasn't time for breakfast. I waited ages for the bus but eventually arrived at the town centre. After signing on, collecting my money and then I had to wait in a long queue for another bus to take me to the rent office to pay my rent. I started feeling dizzy so I made my way to the staff entrance of a bank where I blacked out. A girl took me to the office where the staff were very kind and gave me a cup of tea. I told them that I had dashed out with nothing to eat. I was then able to catch the bus to the rent office to pay my rent.

Chapter 4

A Bad Accident

One early evening in my flat I was listening to my radio, I didn't have a television or a telephone then, and was feeling very tired. I had my back to the paraffin heater to try to get warm and I can't remember properly what happened next. My dressing gown must have caught fire but I managed to put the flames out and get onto my bed and fallen asleep. When I woke up my legs were bloody and I couldn't walk. I had burnt the skin off the backs of my legs. I managed to get on my knees and crawled to the front door next to mine. I rattled the letter box, the lady living there saw me on the floor and I explained what had happened. Neither of us had a telephone so she went to the caretaker downstairs. He phoned for an ambulance which took me to hospital. They just bandaged my legs and sent me back to my flat. The next day I rattled my neighbour's letter box again and told her what happened. She gave me something to eat and told the caretaker. I went to the hospital again and again they just bandaged my legs.

I was waiting in reception for an ambulance when a thought came to me. I phoned the police asked for a message to be taken to my parent's address saying that their daughter had had an accident and was waiting at the hospital reception. I seemed to be waiting for ages for the ambulance to come but maybe it was just as well for

I saw my parents walking towards me. I told them what had happened so when the ambulance arrived, instead of returning to Kirkby, I went to live with my father and mother again.

I went to the royal Infirmary where they put me on liquids for nine weeks. This meant I could ask any of the nursing staff for a drink of milk or orange juice or anything anytime I wanted all round the clock. If the skin on the backs of my legs did not heal I would have to have a skin graft. Fortunately, the skin did heal but made my toes feel tight. I had to have the big toe on my left foot amputated.

It was about this time that my sister Georgina got married to Chris. She was a teacher and they now have two grown up children, Peter and Selina. Last year Selina married Paul. My brother George married Liz and they have two grown up children, Lisa and Jenny. Jenny is married and has two children, Michael and Lilley.

Chapter 5

Adjustments

After I had been living with my parents for a while we got a ground floor flat on medical grounds because my parents were only living in rooms.

Mrs Levy lived in the flat next door to us. She was a widow and she had a bad heart. She had one son who was married but they couldn't have children. Mrs Levy said I could visit her anytime for a chat, which I used to do. When my two nieces were small and they came to visit my parents they used to collect wild flowers, put them in a bunch and give them to my mother. My father worked in the betting shop. My mother pushed me in my wheelchair to the shops. I saw Mrs Levy's son who said his mother had gone to hospital to have a heart operation but had died before the operation.

After about a month, a middle aged married couple moved in next door. They were very nice people. One Christmas I thought I would give my mother a break so I spent the Christmas at a Leonard Cheshire home. I shared a room with an old disabled lady. In the lounge was a big Xmas tree, a big table full of wine and other drinks and sandwiches and mince pies. A vicar came round to give us all a present. I got talcum powder. When the lounge was empty and it was getting dark, I could see through the long french windows. There was snow for miles around and not a soul or a building in sight.

I had a drink and fell asleep by the fireplace. When I woke up I was scared – I couldn't see! I could hear them all going into the dining room for their breakfast. I called out and one of the staff came to me and stayed for a while. Then, thank God, my sight came back.

Then another time my mother came with me to the dental hospital.There was a big rocking horse in reception for children to play on. I was only going there for a check up but a lady in a white jacket came up to me and stuck a needle in my gum. I must have passed out as the next thing I remember was dentists standing around me trying to wake me up and my mother looking very worried. I told the dentists about the lady in the white jacket and one asked "Did you see the name on her badge?" I said "No, I didn't have time."

Another time one summer my mother and I went on a trip on the Royal Iris ferry. It started raining so we went below for a coffee. My wheelchair folds up so we got the bus back home. As I stepped from the bus into my wheelchair my mother said "Look, your father is peeping round the curtain to see when we are getting off the bus." Our block of flats was not very far from the bus stop.

The lady who lived next door in the block of flats had some sad news. She said she had gone into the kitchen to get her husband a coffee and when she returned he had died in the armchair.

Chapter 6

Finding a New Place

After a while I got myself a ground floor council flat to give my mother a break and to be independant. After a while it was a nightmare. Outside my flat was just like hills. There were no other buildings, only the block of flats. One winter the wind was that strong my bathroom window was completely blown in. It wasn't repaired for two days. I got no sleep as I was frightened to go to the bathroom as the window faced the outside. Anybody could have got in and nobody would have heard me crying for help. There were lots of stray dogs around there and they could have got in.

I phoned my social worker and she came to see me. I told her everything and she said she knew of a spastic residential home but they took in all kinds of disabled people. It was Angers House in Penny Lane and she said I could go on a month's trial just to see if I liked it. I didn't have to stay if I didn't want to. So I went and shared a room with two spastic old ladies. I told the social worker I did not want to go back to that flat. I was in Angers House for four years. My mother used to visit me once a week. There were also men there as well. Some were violent, some took fits but I didn't tell my mother this.

My mother used to phone me every Tuesday. One Tuesday she phoned me and said "Your father is passing blood and is in hospital." Then I had to go into hospital myself to get a lump removed from my right foot. I had the district nurse for two years because it kept discharging. The matron let me home for weekend leaves to stay with my mother.

One Sunday my mother came back after visiting hospital and said "Your father has passed away." I told the matron and I went back to live with my mother. She used to take his photograph into her bedroom every night and I could hear her saying prayers. Then she had to go to hospital to have her gullet stretched and then she came home.

Then we had a nice day out at Southport. I remembered a few years back when my mother and father and I went on a weeks holiday to Southport we stayed at a nice hotel. We went to the theatre and saw famous comedian Dickie Henderson and then we went to a nice cafe and had a beautiful three course meal. Mother paid for the lot.

Years back in 1976 my parents and I went to Devon. The advert was out of a psychic newspaper. As well as owning the guest house, Mr and Mrs Gee also did healing. I had to phone the train station to let them know we were coming because I was in a wheelchair. It was a six hour journey on the train. It was built on slopes when we got there we didn't know. we didn't have a motorcar so my father used to push me in my wheelchair up the slopes. He was fit then. We saw the model village. There's a model village in Southport as well.

Chapter 7

A Final Move and Goodbye

EVENTUALLY we all got told the flats were coming down to make way for a bigger road, but they were keeping the houses up. We didn't get much notice. Everything was quick. My brother's wife Liz had to buy some cheap curtains quick and put them up before it went dark. Electric and gas had to be notified and we had to make sure the telephone was working and electricity and heating switched on. When the landlord came next day I said, "I've posted about fifty letters to different places to notify change of address. This is number 4."

The landlord looked at me, "You're not number 4, you are plot 4." So I had to write to all these places again to say I had made a mistake and give them the right number.

My mother and I moved into this bungalow in 1996 and the lady called Julie who lived next door to us in the flats also lives next door to us in the bungalows.

But my mother Debbie kept having falls. One day she went to the shops and the wind blew her against an iron grid. She had her shoulder broken and went into hospital. I used to visit her in a wheelchair taxi and I'd spend hours at her bedside even if she was asleep. I'd phone for a wheelchair taxi from the hospital even in the winter, come back home, phone the hospital and ask the night staff to tell my mother that I had arrived at home because she used to worry.

She got better and came home then slipped and broke her hip. She was in hospital for weeks and passed away on February 1, 2000, which is also my nephew's birthdate. The lady next door, Julie, when she phones me she says, "I don't half miss your mum" and she cries. She says, "I talk to your Mum's photo every morning when I get up, also her husband's photo."

I phoned the chapel of rest and asked if it was all right to visit my mother in a wheelchair taxi. They said it was, so I got a wheelchair taxi down to Breck Road where a young man from the funeral place came to meet me and wheeled me back to it. I sat with my mother for hours just talking to her as if she was still alive. I even said I was hoping to win on the lottery. I said I missed her and I told her Julie next door misses her. I said I'd probably see her again one day. The young man appeared at the door. "Do you want a cup of tea?"

I said, "No, I would be all right." I phoned for a wheelchair taxi and went home. Later on in the week I visited her again.

I have called this poem *God's Heaven* just like John Lennon's song called *Imagine*. Imagine God's heaven where the sun always shines. People are never ill, anybody can have their own house or cottage wherever they wanted, no repairs needed, no bills to pay, that is what I would call heaven.

GOD'S HEAVEN

I have read that we have lived many lifetimes before
If that is true, were we rich or poor?
Happy or sad?
Good or bad?
Black or white or yellow or brown?
Always with a smile or always with a frown?
Somebody's Mum or Dad?
Or a girl or a lad?
What country? What town? What street?
Past friends do we again meet?
If this is part of God's plan
He must be very clever
Will we ever see Him in heaven high?
Beyond the sky
Like when we dream
We don't plan the scene
We can't complain to God and say that
Was a lousy dream give us back our money
He would probably think we were just
Being rather funny.

This poem is called *Demolition*. It is about changes in our lives that we don't make. The flats came down to make way for a bigger road but they kept the houses up in the road. Since moving to the new bungalows they're our new neighbours on the other side of the street in houses. They are very nice, we still keep in touch with neighbours from the old street which means we have more friends. We still send Xmas cards. They say God works in mysterious ways.

DEMOLITION

I used to live in a ground floor flat
Then we all got told the flats have got to come down
Now we all live in bungalows nearer the town
They kept the houses with their beautiful
back gardens full of flowers
But now we have back gardens full of trees and
flowers which are ours
We didn't have gardens in the flats
But in our back gardens now
There's plenty of magpies and pussycats
Then the odd firework can be heard in the big field
As it gets nearer bonfire night
Out come the firemen to put out the fire in the field
Gives everyone a fright
Thank God for the rain
I suppose cats and dogs all think the same.